1

Printed in the United States of America

ISBN-13: 978-0692439883 (Genres Publishing)

ISBN-10: 0692439889

A 30 Day Workbook

Guide to Becoming an Entrepreneur

CONSTANCE HICKS

Table of Contents

The ABC's to Becoming an Entrepreneur Workbook

This workbook is designed to assist you in stepping out in FAITH and making PROGRESS as your start this journey of entrepreneurship. I hope my inspirational readings in my book, The ABC's to Becoming An Entrepreneur, 30 Day Workbook, Guide to Becoming an Entrepreneur, and Entrepreneur Seminars encourage and inspire you to operate in your sweet spot. I hope you pursue your dream, and I pray that your business is successful. I admire you for stepping out in FAITH, believing in yourself, and rolling up your sleeves to put in the work. FAITH without WORK is dead. To those in which much is given, much is required. You and only YOU can represent the SUCCESS of your business.

You must remember that great success has a small beginning. You must stay hungry in your hustle and prepare, plan, and be persistent. You must dance into your destiny, imagine your company, foresee your vision, and challenge yourself to leave contented as you stay committed. Move yourself from a comfortable to an uncomfortable position so that you can achieve success. The road to success is never relaxed. As an entrepreneur, you learn to find calm in the uneasiness.

You are a CEO, CFO, Entrepreneur, and a Small Business Owner. You must do it, believe it, see it, and trust in yourself. You were born to win. You will not give up or give in, but you will give it your all. Do not procrastinate another day, week or month. You will get it. *Let's go.*

Week 1

Day 1

You need to purchase and start a journal so you can write your thoughts down every day. Ideas will come to you at any given moment so you must be ready to write them down. Your journal should be your business bible and carried with you 24 hours a day.

What are your thoughts about the product or service you want to brand?

Day 2

Today, set aside 15-30 minutes and write something in your journal in regards to your ideas about your product or service. For example, write down a short-term goal with a realistic due date.

Day 3

Think about your passion. *What is your passion? What do you like to do? What is fun for you?* Answer these questions in detail.

Day 4

Do you see your passion bringing in some type of revenue? Can you make a profit from this passion?

Day 5

What is the name of your product or service? Think about your brand's name in print? Close your eyes. Can you see your brand's name in magazines, on billboards, or in stores?

Day 6

Describe your emotional state in your journal. How do you feel thus far about your branding your passion (product or service)?

Day 7

Spend some time with yourself and read one page of the inspirational reading in my book, The ABC's to Becoming an Entrepreneur. Now write down something that you recently did to get you one step closer to launching your product or service.

Week 2

Day 1

Choose a day to conduct research on your name. Make sure you google your name to see if it has been trademarked. If not then you need to consider getting your name trademarked. Check sites like (Legal Zoom, United States Patent and Trademark, or Trademarks).

Day 2

Today, take some time out to conduct research about your product or service. Check to see if this product or service is already being offered to the public. If so, contact the company in person or call them. Ask questions and write down the information below.

Day 3

Go back and read another page of my book, The ABC's to Becoming an Entrepreneur, and write down one word that encourages or inspires you to continue to pursue your dream.

Day 4

Draw a picture or sketch of your product or service even if you are not an artist. Use your imagination and draw it to the best of your ability.

Day 5

Call or meet with two or three friends or colleagues, who you trust and value their opinion and share with them your brand's name. Ask them to share their honest thoughts with you about your brand's name. It is constructive criticism. Write down their feedback.

Day 6

Visit social media to see what your competitors are doing to market their business and write down ideas to help you launch your brand.

Day 7

Start a blog about your brand's name via social media to get feedback. If you are not comfortable discussing your brand's name find a creative way to describe your business in order to get continuous feedback.

Week 3

Day 1

Once you are comfortable with your brand's name, the next step is to decide if you will operate as an LLC or a sole proprietor. Visit your local courthouse and pay for your DBA.

Day 2

Think about your budget. How much do want to invest? How much start-up capital are you willing to risk? Write down a realistic dollar amount.

Day 3

If you do not have the startup capital there are other avenues to explore. Consider the option of taking on a silent investor or business partner. This may be a great alternative if you are uncomfortable stepping out solo with your project. If you are comfortable however, then you may consider a small business loan. Check with your local financial resources. For example, the bank, Small Business Council or Small Business Administration, etc. *What did you discover?*

Day 4

Visit a local small business organization to consult with you about your business idea. Think about your projected budget, potential income, and overall business plan. If you are comfortable and have some knowledge about creating a business plan, then you can create your own. Have someone review it to check for information that you may have omitted.

Day 5

Write questions on social media or start a daily blog to engage your followers in a dialogue about your product or service. Think about them as your potential clients and have an answer to their problems.

Day 6

Write another short term goal for you to achieve. What steps will you take to attain this short-term goal?

Day 7

Now, let us think outside the box. Write a long-term goal with a realistic deadline. Describe the steps you need to accomplish in order to achieve this long-term goal. For example, my goal is to do a soft launch for my brand in 6 to 9 months from today. My plans are to _____.

Week 4

Day 1

Start mind mapping your ideas to narrow down the best beneficial route for launching your product or service.

Day 2

Conduct a written or oral survey with co-workers, friends or church members to see if there is a demand for your product or service. Write down some of the results.

Day 3

Reflect on what steps you have completed thus far and what steps remain. Describe how you feel about your entrepreneur journey so far.

Day 4

Today, visit with a small business banker to discuss opening a small business account. If you are comfortable and ready, then take the time to open up your small business account. Find a bank that requires a low minimum to open your account, for example, a $25.00-$100.00 minimum is a great limit to open up your account. Which bank did go with and why? If you are not able to open up an account yet then give yourself a deadline to do that as soon as possible.

Day 5

Start thinking about your brand's logo and write down ideas about your brand's logo.

Day 6

Make calls to get estimates from a company or freelancer to design your logo. If you are working with a smaller budget and cannot afford to get one designed, you can visit Google to help you with images for your logo. Sometimes you can find logo images via Internet for a less expensive price as opposed to a graphic designer. Keep in mind that the logo images are limited and they may vary. They may not be the exact image you had in mind but it may be close to it. What did you find out? What do you think?

Day 7

Okay, now you are off to a GREAT start. You should know if you're ready to launch your product or service. Your ideas should be illustrated in a mind map, you should have some marketing ideas, and you should have your name or logo. Summarize where you are today, at this very moment, in regards to your brand in detail.

Progression Tracker:

www.ingramcontent.com/pod-product-compliance
Lightning Source LLC
Chambersburg PA
CBHW070810220326
41520CB00055B/7118